THE
ANGEL OF ANTIOCH

Daniel Molyneux

ANGEL OF ANTIOCH BOOKS

THE ANGEL OF ANTIOCH

By Daniel Molyneux

www.angelofa.com

Copyright © 2014 by Daniel R. Molyneux

All rights reserved.

Angel of Antioch Books

PO Box 1094

Casper, WY 82602

Daniel Molyneux is available to speak at your event, contact him at: pastordanmolyneux@yahoo.com

Library of Congress Control Number: 2015900093

ISBN-10: 1507667272

ISBN -13: 978-1507667279

Cover illustration by John Singer Sargent, public domain

Author photograph © 2013 by Daniel R. Molyneux

Library Edition: January 31, 2015

DEDICATION

To the millions of martyrs who have been persecuted for their faith throughout history. I also dedicate this book to my children and my wonderful wife.

Table of Contents

ACKNOWLEDGMENTS:

If not for the example of many spiritual giants this book would never have been written. The Way of a Pilgrim, recounting a Christian's spiritual pilgrimage across Russia, has profoundly influenced my faith. John Bunyan's The Pilgrim's Progress, an allegorical journey through life's challenges, has deepened the spiritual path of millions, including mine. Brother Lawrence's The Practice of the Presence of God, demonstrates the holiness of even menial tasks and the importance of the lowliest servant.

I thank Wm. Paul Young, Brennan Manning, Paul Coelho, Elie Wiesel, Corrie Ten Boom, Kahlil Gibran, Brother Andrew, Hank Paulson and C.S. Lewis for their spiritual classics: The Shack, The Ragamuffin Gospel, The Alchemist, Night, The Hiding Place, The Prophet, God's Smuggler, Beyond the Wall and The Screwtape Letters.

Thank-you to the faculties of Fuller, Austin and Concordia seminaries, and of Rocky Mountain College who shared their great knowledge and faith.

Many thanks to the wonderful spiritual leaders who have taught me so much: Clarke and Pat Vestal, Andy Dearman, Don Bobb, Bob Shelton, Pete Hendrick, Chuck Tanner, Dan Davis, Stan Simmons, Scott Ross, Hank Paulson, Bill and Nona Baker, Bob Holmes, Ron and Nancy Kapalka, Pete Wagner, Chuck Kraft, Mark and

Sharon Zehender, Bob Newton, Lon Haack, Dan Ritter, Russ Sommerfeld, Joel Biermann, Steve and Rita Wagner, and Mark Cutler.

Thank-you Martin Luther King, Jim Reeb and the countless others who have willingly sacrificed their lives in the pursuit of justice.

Most importantly I thank God, the origin of all that exists, in whom we trust, the author and source of all truth and creativity.

INTRODUCTION

Reformers vs. Religious Leaders

A state of perpetual conflict exists between institutional religious leaders, and itinerate spiritual outsiders who wield charismatic authority but lack organizational approval.

Israel's kings, priests and Levites were called to lead God's Children into deeper relationship with their Lord. Instead Israel's institutional authorities were often deaf to Yahweh's voice and led the people away from God.

Whether prophets, apostles, saints or reformers, Abraham, Moses, Elijah, John the Baptist, Francis of Assisi, Martin Luther, Tolstoy, Martin Luther King Jr., Aleksandr Solzhenitsyn or a thousand others, these charismatic outsiders suddenly appear throughout Scripture and history, calling priests, kings, tyrants, politicians and all people to a renewed and deeper relationship with God. In the name of the Lord God Almighty, they disrupt the status quo and challenge the institutional authorities who have gone astray.

The Setting

Alexander the Great conquered a vast domain that included Jerusalem and the land promised to the Children of Israel. Dying suddenly in 323 BCE, and leaving no descendants, Alexander's Greek generals divided and ruled the Macedonian Empire.

Seleucus seized control of Syria and Babylonia, founding Antioch as the imperial capital. The city's first inhabitants were local peasants, Greeks, and Jewish mercenaries serving in Seleucus' army. Over the decades, a large, prosperous and influential Jewish community developed.

At its peak, Antioch was the third largest city in the world. Having a population of 500,000 souls, it was surpassed in size and importance only by the cities of Rome and Alexandria.

By 200 BCE numerous synagogues had been established in the Seleucid capital. The most important was the Great Synagogue, noted by the historian Josephus for its beauty and grandeur. More than a mere synagogue, the Great House of Prayer conducted worship and rituals adapted from the Temple. Antiochean Jews continued to revere Jerusalem as God's special place of blood atonement, but sacrifices of praise, incense and prayer were offered on a daily basis in the Great House.

Antioch's Jewish residents and synagogues were ruled by an Archon, a member of the Zadok priesthood. He was aided in his duties by a Council of Elders consisting of Levite representatives from around the city. Additional religious leaders were called teachers or clerics.

Greek culture was dominant in Antioch, including its polytheistic religion honoring Zeus as "king of the gods." Tyche, the mistress of fortune and luck, was Antioch's patron goddess. In spite of this, many gentiles were drawn to the Jewish religion.

Antiochean Jews did not live separately in a ghetto, but dwelled alongside their gentile neighbors, mingling with them to a greater degree than in any other city actively seeking converts among the Greeks. Language was not an obstacle, because all prayer, worship and even the study of Jewish Scripture was done in Greek, not Aramaic or Hebrew.

Although few gentiles submitted to circumcision or fully obeyed the Torah's dietary rules, nonetheless many worshipped Yahweh, were allowed entrance into the Great House and other synagogues, and were respectfully called "God-fearers" by their Jewish friends (Greek - phoboumenoi ton Theon). This gave the Archon and Council of Elders additional political influence with the Emperor.

Circumstances began to deteriorate for the Jews in 175 BCE, when Antiochus Epiphanes (Antiochus IV) became emperor. A fierce advocate of Greek culture, he viewed Jewish religion to be barbaric and incompatible with "civilized" Hellenic society.

Seven years after taking the throne, Epiphanes desecrated the Jerusalem Temple by placing a statue of Zeus in the Holy of Holies and sacrificed pigs upon its altar. The Emperor abolished Jewish worship, the observance of Sabbaths and festivals, outlawed circumcision and destroyed copies of the Scriptures.

Epiphanes forced Jews to worship Zeus and to eat pork that had been sacrificed to the idol. Those refusing were executed. Anyone who circumcised their newborn son was killed, along with the child.

The events recorded in this book take place during Antiochus Epiphanes' reign, but before his desecration of the Jerusalem Temple - 1100 years after the Prophet Moses and 200 years before the crucifixion of Yeshua Ha'Mashiach (Jesus the Christ).

ONE:
A Stranger Arrives

On a sunny morn in early spring the smell of flower blossoms filled the air, enveloping me in the sweet scent of God's creation. Arriving at the Great House for Sabbath prayers, I passed through the massive bronze doors, stone columns standing guard at the entrance on either sides - the Pillar of Wisdom to the left and the Pillar of Truth on the right.

To the Children of Israel living in Antioch, the Great House of Prayer was the most holy place in all the world, other than the Lord's Temple in Jerusalem.

Entering inside, the scent of flowers was overpowered by the pungent smell of incense, turning my thoughts to the Lord, reminding me that I stood on holy ground. Existing betwixt and between heaven and earth, the Great House seemed far removed from this physical world, a sanctuary where erring human beings dared to approach the Holy Lord through faith, repentance, sacrifice and prayer.

Once assembled, the devout faced towards Jerusalem. Worship began with outstretched arms in the manner prescribed by ancient tradition. The Archon and Levites led a cappella psalms of praise, music reverberating off the ceiling, stone walls and marble floor.

Worship progressed until the appointed time for Holy Scripture to be read to the assembly. All bowed and then sat down upon the floor as the Archon retrieved the Torah from its place of honor. Carrying the scroll of the Lord's Law down the stone steps and into the midst of the assembly, he searched for a man of God's own choosing. Turning in whichever direction the Spirit led him, the Archon looked for a person emanating the Lord's anointing. After a few moments he handed the scroll to a man I had never seen before.

Standing up from his place, the stranger ascended the platform to read the passage of the day. Placing God's Law upon its lectern for reading, he did not unroll the scroll but began to recite the appointed passage by heart, speaking each word perfectly, without glancing at the written text.

After speaking the Scripture he explained its meaning, uttering the most eloquent and profound words I had ever heard. Holy Wisdom (Greek - Hagia Sophia) flowed from the stranger's mouth, as though she had made her home within his heart, bringing forth a flood of insight with each syllable he spoke.

The man's words were profound yet divisive, kind but hard, gentle and filled with power. Wielding his words like a sharp sword, he divided the assembly in two. Some worshippers displayed expressions of awe, amazement and joy upon their faces while listening to the stranger's teaching. Other faces were contorted in looks of dismay and anger.

Upon finishing his lesson, the stranger returned to his place among the assembly. When Sabbath prayers ended, he walked into the crowd that was filling the aisle. Before anyone could say a word to him, the stranger disappeared as quickly as he had come, vanishing in the blink of an eye.

Walking out of the Great House, discussion about the man rang throughout the courtyard among the worshippers. Many expressed a fervent desire to hear more of the stranger's words, agreeing that such wisdom could come only from the Mouth of God. But no one knew his identity, where the man had come from or where he lived.

Others expressed contempt for the stranger, ridiculing his clothing, appearance and teaching, comparing his words to those of a fool, expressing their desire to never see or hear him again.

News of the stranger quickly spread throughout Antioch. Speculation about him multiplied among the Children of Israel, God-fearers and even among the Greeks.

On the next Sabbath the Great House was more crowded than usual. Rumors about this mystery man led many to attend Sabbath prayer out of curiosity, having the uncertain hope that the stranger might return and speak once more, if not during worship, then at least in the courtyard afterwards. Some had already started calling him "The Teacher", even though no one knew anything about him.

Sabbath prayers began. Many surveyed the congregation searching for a glimpse of the man. Worship progressed. Once again the Archon brought the Sacred Scripture down into the assembly, handing it to a person near the center of the congregation. When he stood up, all could see it was the same stranger who had spoken the Sabbath before. Yet again he spoke the appointed passage by heart, not looking at the text even once.

When he finished the Scripture, overcome with enthusiasm I shouted, "Teacher, tell us the meaning of God's Holy Word."

Another said, "Yes Teacher, give us freely from God's Wisdom that we might drink and be filled."

Words dripped off his tongue like honey, sweet and satisfying, filling the House of Prayer with what felt like a warm woolen blanket, soothing my soul. While he spoke, I closed my eyes allowing the stranger's words to envelope me, not wanting anything to distract from his insights.

Upon opening my eyes I was startled by grimaces of displeasure and stares of anger etched deeply into many faces, especially upon the Archon and honored ones serving on the platform, the clerics and elders who daily study God's Word and teach the Way of Submission. Their faces were contorted in expressions of disapproval, irritation and animosity.

When I turned away from the religious leaders and gazed at the crowd of common but devout worshippers, many appeared as pleased by the stranger's words as I was, as though they were enveloped in a cloud of ecstasy.

The man returned to his place in the midst of the assembly. At the end of prayers, he walked into the crowd and quickly disappeared, like the week before.

Gossip about the stranger became ridiculous. Some Greeks speculated he might be Phoebus the Writer of Dreams. Others thought he was the bodily incarnation of Hermes, the winged messenger. A Persian said the man was Zoroaster come again.

A devout God-fearer who faithfully attended the Great House said, "Perhaps this stranger is one of the Almighty's Holy Angels. No mere human could be entrusted with such words from the Oracle of God. Perhaps he is not a man, but is the Angel Gabriel in disguise, sent to encourage us with God's Word, just as the Angel was sent to the prophet in Babylon. No man of flesh and blood can appear and disappear as this stranger does."

A Levite said to a group of religious teachers gathered round him, "This stranger only appears to be a man. He is a desert demon, a messenger of Belial sent to plant seeds of confusion, leading the faithful to their destruction." Many clerics shook their heads in agreement.

Some of the faithful speculated the man was a prophet. Others hoped he might be the Anointed One prophesied in Scripture, predicted to appear in the Last

Days to crush the head of the Serpent and free the Children of Israel from the tyrants who have oppressed them.

That no one knew anything about the stranger only added to his fame, as a frenzy of excitement grew among the people of Antioch. The mystery surrounding this man merely fed everyone's fantasies about him.

Like a beautiful, perfect and newly cut piece of marble before the sculptor's chisel has touched the stone, each person imagined the figure they longed to see, visualizing the fulfillment of whatever dream they desired. Although no one could agree upon his true identity or importance, for good or ill, all were intrigued by him nonetheless. Discussion about the man was on everyone's lips. As days passed, the stories and speculation became ever more outlandish.

When the next Sabbath arrived, every nook and cranny of the Great House was filled with the rich and poor, the powerful as well as powerless, filled to overflowing.

Along the walls stood gentiles who were easy to recognize, but no one dared ask them to leave, members of the Emperor's Secret Guard whom everyone feared. Their traits varied: some short and others tall, skinny or fat, handsome and ugly, young or old. Each was dressed in disguise, but none could hide their true identity. Displaying grey-grim faces, their bodies were draped in drab attire - boring, formal, uptight and harsh. Each possessed the same lifeless eyes displaying eagerness to carry out their violent deeds without mercy, whenever the order is given.

TWO:
Division in the Assembly

Prayer began. When it came time to read the Holy Scriptures, the Sacred Scroll was handed to a man near the front. The stranger stood to read the lesson once again. Like the previous two Sabbaths, he recited the passage from memory and then explained its meaning.

After finishing his teaching, leaving the platform and about to take his place in assembly, a young man shouted, "Teacher, tell us the truth."

"What truth do you desire to hear?" asked the stranger.

"God's Truth," said the man.

Examining him carefully the stranger said, "But my son, you do not desire the Lord's Truth."

"How can you say such a thing Teacher? Of course I want to hear the truth. Like all people, I want to know the Word of God."

"You are mistaken my son," said the stranger. "Men and women do not naturally desire the Almighty's Truth. The Lord whispers silent words that are alien and unpleasant to the human ear."

The young man was offended. Storming out of the Great House he shouted, "Who does this vagabond think he is, to say that I do not want to hear God's Truth? Who is this man to sit in judgment of me?"

Another asked, "Teacher, what is true and perfect religion?"

The stranger said, "My dear friend, religion by itself is of little value."

"How can you call yourself a religious teacher and say such a thing?" asked the man.

"Friend, I do not call myself a teacher, and most assuredly I do not call myself religious. Search your heart for the reason my answer upsets you." replied the stranger.

The man protested, "But Teacher, religion is the way we come to know the Lord and how we learn about God's Commands."

"What is your name my dear child?"

"Abraham," said the man.

"You have a good name my son," said the stranger. "Be true to your name. Father Abraham had great faith in the Almighty. When the Lord spoke, Abraham believed. Even though he was old and childless, when the Mighty One promised him children and countless descendants, Abraham trusted God and the promise that was given to him."

"But Abraham was religious," said the man.

"Friend, most religion is a human creation. Faith in the Mighty One is what matters most. The Lord God called Abraham to separate himself from the religious idolatry of his homeland and ancestors. Abraham worshipped God in the wilderness using rough unfinished stones for an altar. Father Abraham's trust in the Almighty was his religion. But most religious ritual is birthed from human superstition - spells and incantations devised to manipulate celestial forces to do the will of women and men."

The man asked, "But what about the traditions handed down to us by our ancestors, generation to generation? The ancient traditions show us the path to God."

The stranger replied, "Religious traditions can be good or evil, beneficial or harmful, like all human inventions. The Torah given through Moses is the only religious tradition required. I do not tell you to abandon your rituals and religious traditions. But I warn you not to confuse human-made religion with true faith in God."

"Then tell me, Teacher, how does one obtain true faith in the Lord?"

"Ah my son, this is a very fine question. Faith arrives when a person comes to the end of themselves. When one despairs of learning and loses all hope of earning the Lord's favor, when a person tires of their own foolish knowledge and becomes disillusioned with all human endeavors, this is when true faith beckons. When a woman or man comes to the end of the World and its false wisdom, this is when true faith calls, faith in the One and Only, the Lord Almighty."

The man said, "This is a hard lesson Teacher. Who can accept it?"

"The Lord cannot be understood by the human mind or intellect," said the stranger. "If mere human beings could comprehend the Mighty One, then He would not be the Source, the Origin, the Creator, the Lord God Almighty.

"God cannot be seen by human eyes. To experience the Lord's presence is to be enveloped in a dense cloud and unable to see. Within the foggy darkness a silent whisper is uttered into one's ear, bringing both joy and fear. In silent hearing and blind seeing the Lord's presence is revealed.

"The Almighty dwells beyond all that is. When a person is surrounded by the Lord's presence, embraced by Life itself, a divine revelation is revealed to human awareness, an assurance that death and evil shall be utterly overcome and destroyed. While held tightly in the Lord's Arms a spring gushes forth from God's Spirit, bathing one in the waters of Life. In God's presence is both heaven and joy, dispelling darkness, depression and doubt, overcoming the fog of this frail and fragile World.

"The Lord is like lightening. Startled by its appearance and momentarily blinded by the brightness of the flash, when the lightning strikes, a person is either destroyed or jolted to new life.

"The One True God is encountered in a cloud of unknowing after all hope of finding the Lord is abandoned. This is when a small piece of the Divine Essence is shown to a woman or man. This is when faith arrives, given as a gift from the Almighty. At the moment of surrender, the Lord's silent voice loudly cries out, 'Believe!' When one responds to the Mighty One's quiet call, and in their heart truly does believe, this is true faith in the One True God."

Many in the crowd had dark looks of confusion and disapproval drawn upon their faces, like they were held tightly in the grip of constipation. Some shook their heads violently at the stranger's words, as though he spoke gibberish, insane musings, or the mutterings of someone possessing a demon.

A man dressed in clerical robes came forward walking towards the stranger, one of the Archon's assistants. He spoke in a loud voice saying, "Why are you disrupting our prayers in this Holy House? Worship is not yet concluded, but you continue to squirt your diseased words. You are no longer on the platform or explaining the Torah. Who gave you permission to speak your confused speculations disrupting holy worship? You are not dressed in a teacher's robes, nor have you been assigned to this Holy Place. Who gave you authority to speak beyond your appointed time and position?"

The stranger replied, "My son, I will tell you by what authority I speak. But first tell me, who gave you authority to teach and to be a religious leader?"

With his head held high the Levite said, "I studied for years under the greatest and most learned Levites of Jerusalem. His Holiness, Archon Menelaus, personally gave me license to serve the Almighty and to teach the Lord's people here in our city. His Honor Menelaus officially assigned me to this Great House of Prayer."

The stranger said, "My son, did the Lord call you to be the Almighty's mouthpiece and to speak on His behalf?"

"Archon Menelaus laid hands on me personally," said the Levite, "giving me his blessing, charging me to preach and to teach God's commands in this Holy House."

"But my son," said the stranger, "did the Mighty One call you to preach and to teach in God's name?"

Becoming increasingly agitated and angry the Levite said, "Are you deaf or merely dull? Did you not hear my answer already? Must I repeat it for you yet again? How many times must I tell you? Clearly you have not been properly educated in God's Law or been approved by holy leaders. You speak differently, like one poorly instructed in religious truth. You have no license. You are clearly heterodox, a heretic, a false teacher, a false prophet, having no right to teach in this Holy Place, polluting the righteous with perverse Greek and Persian philosophies." Then the cleric turned and left to find the Emperor's

Regiment of Guardians, those who maintain order among Antioch's various temples and their surrounding courts. As he left, the Levite shouted that he was going to have the stranger removed from the Great House of Prayer by force.

Undeterred others wanted to hear more from the stranger. One asked, "Teacher, why do religious people do so many evil things?"

The stranger said, "All people do evil and sinful things, including those who are deeply religious, even those who have great faith. To believe otherwise is to believe a lie. The Almighty alone is perfect and does no evil thing. To expect people of faith to be without sin and to do no evil, is to expect perfection from the deeply flawed and imperfect. To believe that religious people will act like God is laughable. Was the Prophet Moses without sin or Father Abraham?

"As a dog returns to its own vomit to devour it once again, so too each woman and man returns to their own evil deeds to partake of them once more. The Almighty can and does change the human heart, but even a transformed man or woman retains their sinful flesh, still in need of the Lord's help, forgiveness and mercy.

"Those who reject faith in the Lord because of the evil deeds of religious people, fail to understand their own sin and the pervasive nature of evil in this fallen World. More importantly, they fail to comprehend the Lord's mercy and forgiveness. If they do not understand this World's evil that surrounds them, how can they hope to comprehend the goodness and generosity of God, or have faith in the Lord's promise of deliverance from darkness, sin and death?

"True faith is trust in the Lord. It is not faith in religious people or religious institutions. The Almighty alone is perfect, merciful and just. All others will deeply disappoint, hurt and betray you.

"No fallen human being born into this World is immune to the allure of evil. It is only by the Lord's power that a person escapes the shackles and chains that bind and blind. The Lord alone is without shadow or darkness. The Almighty alone provides a release from evil and death, an escape completed only when one departs this imperfect World. When a Child of God leaves this fallen and earthly flesh, darkness and evil are left behind as well."

A large number of Levites, teachers and clerics from across Syria were in attendance at worship that day, many more than usual. They wanted to hear the stranger because his fame had spread throughout the capital and beyond. When the Levites and clerics heard the Teacher's comments about how deeply flawed all people are, even the religious, many were offended and stood to leave. Regarding themselves as nearly perfect, virtually without sin, the religious leaders thought themselves to be the Lord's favorites and their behavior beyond reproach, viewing themselves to be nearer to God than anything upon this earth.

A Levite said to his colleagues, "We came to hear a man of God, a true religious teacher. Instead all we found is an agnostic, an irreligious apostate who spews nonsense, a reprobate who utters blasphemy against the Lord. He even slanders the righteous, while denying the traditions our ancestors diligently taught us."

The Teacher returned to his place in the assembly and took his seat. Prayer continued. When it finished, a mother drew near to the stranger, together with her young daughter who was gaunt and pencil thin.

The mother said, "Please Teacher, have mercy on my daughter. There is nothing more the physicians can do for her. You are our last hope. I am a widow and she is my only child. I beg you to have mercy upon us. I beg you, pray to the Lord for my daughter's healing."

A loud voice from the middle of the crowd said, "If you truly speak for God, then prove the Lord's Power is with you. Heal this girl."

The stranger replied, "The Lord's Power is only displayed to those who have faith, but it is hidden from all who are prideful and obstinate."

The voice rang out again, "Do you then refuse to prove that God's anointing is upon you?"

"My dear children," said The Teacher, "God has no need to prove anything. The Lord's Power is unleashed through faith. The Almighty performs works of wonder out of compassion and love for the Children of God. Those lacking faith cannot see God's Mighty Works, even when they are clearly displayed. When the Lord's Power is demonstrated through great miracles, people lacking faith cannot perceive them. For the faithless explain away and rationalize every miracle revealed to them. A man only believes what his mind allows him to believe; and a woman only sees what her eyes expect to see.

"If you desire to witness a miracle - in the evening turn west and gaze intently at the sunset. Those who have faith will see God's handiwork in the sky. But the faithless see only sun, clouds and the base elements of nature. When you witness the beauty of an evening sky with its red, purple and orange hues, praise God for the wonders the Lord works each and every day."

A commotion began to spread throughout the Great House as the Archon's Assistant returned through the main entrance. Accompanied by a company of Guardians, he began to make his way down the aisle towards the stranger.

Some in the assembly shouted, "Yes, remove this false teacher from the Holy House, this place of sacred prayer." But others tried to block and hinder the Guardians' advance.

All the while the Emperor's Secret Guard stood by in the shadows, watching the unrest, taking note of all that was happening, but not intervening.

Pushing my way through the crowd, I struggled to catch up to the Teacher. As I drew near, he was bending close to the little girl who was so terribly ill. Gently he placed his hand upon her head and asked, "My precious girl, do you have faith that the Lord will heal you?"

She said in a soft, sweet and innocent voice, "Yes Teacher, I believe."

THREE:

Discourse in the Countryside

The Teacher said to the young girl, "Rejoice my child, for God has answered your prayer."

Then he turned and left the Great House by a side door, leaving the assembly in disarray and dissention. Many shouted curses as he left. Others argued in his defense. Some followed the stranger out of the Great House, including me.

Walking through the streets of Antioch we came to the city's fortified walls. Passing through its gates the Teacher led us into the countryside.

While going up a steep hill we came upon a man who was severely beating his donkey. It was laying upon the road and would not budge because the load was too heavy for the beast to carry.

The Teacher said to its master, "The animal is too small to carry its burden? Why do you make it suffer?"

"What business is it of yours?" said the man. "It is my property. I will do with it as I please."

The Teacher said, "Woe to you for having a hard heart, and dull ears that do not hear the donkey's plea to God for help. Just as you do not hear its cry today, the Lord will not listen to your plea for mercy when you stand before the Almighty on the Last Day. God, the Mighty Judge, will treat you as you have treated this animal."

The Teacher then lifted the donkey's load off its back. Placing it upon his shoulder, he carried it to the top of the hill. Returning to the place where the exhausted animal lay, he gave it a drink from his own water-skin. Gently raising the donkey to its feet, the Teacher slowly led it to the top. There he whispered into the donkey's ear saying, "Take heart my friend. You are a royal mount. Just as King David rode your ancestor into the Holy City, a day will come when one of your descendants will carry the Anointed One through the gates of Jerusalem."

Turning to those of us following, the Teacher said, "If you will not relieve the burden of an animal, slave or lowly servant, you cannot expect God to have mercy upon you. The Lord said through the Prophet Hosea, 'I desire mercy rather than animal sacrifice, and the knowledge of God rather than burnt offerings upon the altar.'"

Continuing down the road, we were soon surrounded by fields of grain. Coming to a peaceful and secluded spot the Teacher stopped. Tall cedars lined the top of the hill, standing watch like silent sentries. He sat upon a large boulder protruding half-way up, while the rest of us sat around him, on the new spring grass that lay across the hillside below, providing a pleasing carpet on which to rest.

I took a seat next to the stranger and said, "Teacher, we know so little about you. What is your name?"

"Why do you wish to know, my friend?"

"It is just simple curiosity, Teacher," I replied.

"My name is not important," said the stranger. "Just as I am of little significance. The only things that truly do matter are the Lord, His Commands, and our brothers and sisters. But to satisfy your curiosity, my name is Elias."

"Teacher, my name is Yutan."

"Welcome Yutan. I am glad you have come on this journey with me," said Elias.

"Teacher, please forgive me for asking so many questions, but why do the Levites and clerics seem to reject your words?"

THE FLOUR JAR:

"Consider this story my friend Yutan. A young woman rode her cart to the market. There she filled a large pottery jar with flour. Placing it in the back of the cart, she made her way home.

"Upon returning her father said, 'Daughter dear, please bake me a small loaf to ease my hunger.'

"The young woman went to carry the jar of flour into the house. Coming to the back of the cart, she found the jar lying upon its side and the flour gone. During her journey down the rocky road, the jar had tipped over, spilling its contents along the way, scattering the flour to the four winds. The jar had been full, but was now empty, leaving no flour to make a loaf to ease her father's hunger."

After pondering the story for a moment I said, "Teacher, I perceive this story is about the Levites, but the meaning escapes me."

"Yes, you are right my friend. It is about some of the Levites. Let me explain. When young, many Levites were eager to be filled with God's Word so they could, in turn, feed many hungry souls. The Almighty filled them to overflowing with the Lord's Sustenance. At first these Levites faithfully gave spiritual food to many, freely distributing the Bread of God.

"But during their years of sojourn in life, the bumps and obstacles of this World confused them, making them dizzy and off balance. Jostled by the trials and potholes of life in this fallen World, their hearts were overturned, spilling the spiritual food the Almighty had given to them. Before long, the Levites were empty vessels, no longer having anything inside their hearts to feed those hungry for God's Word. The Levites appear to be the same vessels on the outside, but inside they are empty, unable to feed those who are starving for the Bread of God. Some Levites are like the jar of flour that fell, spilling its contents to the four winds. Not only are some spiritually empty, they are jealous of anyone who attempts to feed the starving masses with the goodness of God.

THE WINE CASKS:

"Some? What about the other Levites?" I asked.

"Other Levites are like large wooden casks. When the Winemaker came yearly to fill them with new wine they cried out, 'Oh Winemaker, I am full to overflowing and cannot accept another drop.'

For many seasons the Winemaker came to fill the casks. Each year the casks cried out, 'Oh Winemaker, I am full to overflowing and cannot accept another drop.'

At the end of seven-years the Winemaker looked inside every cask. Those that had refused the Maker's wine for seven-seasons were not only empty, but their wood had dried and shriveled making them unable to hold wine; for if filled, the precious liquid would leak through the gaps and cracks, spilling the wine upon the ground and be lost. Such casks are no longer good for anything but to be broken up and thrown onto the Winemaker's fire to warm his house."

"Teacher, I may understand this story," I responded. "The casks that said they are full, but never contained any wine - are they Levites who never had faith in the Lord but only pretended to, religious on the outside but empty inside, never having contained the Lord's Wine within?"

"Well done my good friend. You understand completely," said the Teacher.

THE FULL CASKS:

I asked, "Teacher, are all Levites like the empty flour jar and empty wine casks?"

"No my friend, there is yet another kind of Levite. When asked by the Winemaker to receive wine, these casks gladly accept the Lord's blood red drink that is the essence of life itself. They are filled by the Maker with all the blessed Heavenly Wine they can hold, full to overflowing. These casks are not only Levites, but all people who hunger and thirst for the Lord, all who accept the Wisdom and Grace that the Almighty freely gives.

"The full wine casks are many different kinds of people, great and small, rich and poor, slave and free, near and far, foreign and native, Levites and simple farmers. The title that the World gives to each person matters little to the Lord. What is contained within a man or woman's heart, this is the thing that matters most to God."

DISCOURSE ON THE ALMIGHTY:

A young man said, "Teacher, who is God?"

Elias replied, "'Hear O Israel, the Lord Your God is One.' The Almighty, the Creator, This is the Lord."

The man asked again, "But who is God, Teacher?"

"Human beings cannot fully fathom the Mighty One," said the Teacher. "Men and women cannot even comprehend the cosmos, and are dumbfounded by the tiniest of its living creatures. So how can mere mortals fully grasp the complexity of creation's Maker? Human beings can at best know a small part of who the Lord truly is. Of far greater importance than understanding God, is one's attitude before the Lord. If you desire to know the Almighty, then stand in humble awe of the Creator of all that is. This is where the journey of faith begins.

"If you desire to know what God may be compared to, consider the most loving, caring and compassionate mother or father that you are able to imagine. This is the truest image of the Mystery we call God. And yet the Lord is infinitely greater and more loving than any earthly father or mother. Compassion, mercy, love and forgiveness are the feeble human words that best describe the Almighty. But no earthly word can contain or describe the Mystery that is God; for the Lord is beyond and above all pitiful human understanding or description.

"The Mighty One cannot be fully known by the mind of man. If mere human beings could understand the Almighty, then the Lord would not be God.

"The Mighty One dwells beyond what is. When enveloped in the Lord's Presence, we too are taken outside the finite physical world. Within the embrace of creation's Author, true reality is revealed.

"God's Word gives life, but the World's false utterances bring death.

"The greatest human endeavor is prayer. Through it the Words of God become the words of women and men. In prayer's absence, evil runs amuck, but through fervent faithful prayer and supplication the Lord's deliverance is revealed.

"When one labors to pray, the demons seek to distract and divert from this critical task. Knowing that their dark deeds are overthrown by humble praise and intercession, the devils' chief task is to prevent God's faithful followers from engaging in heartfelt prayer.

"Whenever a person perseveres in prayer, victory results, but it requires great effort, persistence and struggle. The Children of Abraham were in Egypt for six-times-seventy-years before the Almighty redeemed them through the hand of Moses. The Children of Judah were in Babylonian bondage for seventy-years before the Lord's people were returned to the Promised Land. And the time from their return from Babylon until the Anointed One is born shall be seven-times-seventy-years."

ROAD TO DEATH AND THE WAY TO LIFE:

Another said, "Teacher, we have faith in God and all the Lord's promises. What is the next step on the Lord's Path?"

Elias replied, "God calls to each child who walks upon the earth. The Lord's loving and silent Voice beckons us to begin a journey, just as Abraham and Moses were called.

"There are two roads: one descending to darkness and death, and the other leading to Light and Life.

"These are the signs a person is traveling down the dark road to destruction:

"Children of Satan seek to justify their evil deeds and deny their guilt. Ruled by their own whims and lusts, they love lies but hate the Truth. Strangers to faithfulness, honor, generosity, gentleness, patience and compassion, they serve only themselves. Despising the Children of God, they persecute them at every opportunity. Strangers to mercy and forgiveness, they eagerly seek revenge even for the smallest offense. Abusers of children, spouses and parents, they love violence but hate the Lord. Covetous, greedy and hungry for power, they rush into unjust wars of aggression. Raping, pillaging and hoarding spoils, they rejoice over each of their victims. Growing in wealth and rank through their merciless atrocities, human life and suffering mean nothing to them. Quick to shed blood, they hate those who work for peace. Uncaring for the needy, they happily increase the suffering of those in distress. Crooked in all their ways, they extort ransom, take bribes and constantly look for ways to cheat and steal. Degenerate, they pursue every form of selfish pleasure. Having no concern for the damage caused to others, they are driven by their fleshly passions. Having debased minds and lacking a moral compass, they partake in all kinds of immorality. Protectors of the rich, defenders of unjust judges and supporters of corrupt government officials, they sell their loyalty to the highest bidder.

"These are the signs that one is walking upon the Path that leads to Light and Life:

"They treat others as they would like to be treated. Blessing those who curse them and praying for those who hate them, they humbly serve the Lord with all their heart. Generous to the needy, they do not expect to be repaid. Quick to aid widows, orphans, foreigners and those in want, they are full of compassion and care for all. Mindful of their own sins and faults, they are merciful and quick to forgive another's wrong. Pursuers of peace, they do not murder or rashly take up arms. Faithful in all things, they do not betray the trust of others. Honest in all endeavors, they do not steal or take what belongs to another. Concerned about the Lord's Commands, they do not lust after their neighbor's belongings. Lovers of the Truth, they do not lie or bear false witness. Self-controlled in all their ways, they do not speak evil of others, utter curses or spread gossip. Content with what the Lord has provided them, they are not greedy or envious. Praying without ceasing, they intercede for all people, even their enemies. Knowing that God is their protector, they do not fight evil with evil, but overcome evil with good. Full of love for the Lord and their brothers and sisters, they gladly give their lives for others, like lambs sacrificed upon the altar.

"Those who journey through the World in such a way are walking along the Path that leads to Light and Life. Having tossed aside the darkness and chains that blind and bind, in the end they will behold the face of God and dwell with the Lord for timeless ages."

PRAYER:

A young man said, "Teacher, how often must we pray each day? Some Levites tell us to pray three-times, others five."

Elias said, "Yes, five-times if you able, but do not let that be the end of your prayers. Each day you live in this imperfect World, invoke the Lord's Word without ceasing. As you journey through life say silently, 'Praise God; praise God; praise God.' When you do, the clouds of hopelessness will lift and the Lord's Joy will enter into your heart.

"Strive to live in the Almighty's Presence always, remembering that the Lord will never leave you nor forsake you. The Mighty One is with you even in the darkness of despair. Whether you feel near or distant from God, remember that human emotions are misguided, erring and mistaken. The Almighty is always near and never far away. The Lord, the Merciful, the Mighty One is at your right hand, your Deliverer even in the midst of death's dark valley. Do not doubt God, the Lord's nearness or the Almighty's deliverance.

"When you lay down to sleep repeat, 'Praise God, praise God, praise God,' while breathing through your nose. As you do, be conscious of your breathing. Say 'Praise' as you breathe in and 'God' as you breathe out. When you do, peaceful and blissful sleep will descend upon you like a soft blanket.

"Wherever you may be, utter this simple prayer: 'Merciful Lord, have mercy upon me a sinner.' Repeat it continuously without ceasing. As you do life's burdens and worries will begin to fade, like fog dissipating in the morning light. The joy of being in God's Presence will break forth and envelope you in the Lord's loving arms.

"Prayer brings the human heart into agreement with the Mind of God. A prayer's answer arrives when one's heart comes into harmony with the Good and Gracious Will of the Lord.

"Prayer does not change the Mind of God, for only the Almighty knows what is best for each of His precious Children. It is the human heart that is changed and transformed through prayer, converting erring human thought to the Lord's perfect Will and Purpose.

"This imperfect and chaotic World fills the ear with a cacophony of noise and distraction, drowning out the still and quiet Voice of the Lord. But the Word of God is subtle and still, most clearly heard in solitary silence. Worship the Almighty each day. Mediate upon the Lord in quiet solitude. If you do, God's will for your life will be revealed, and the Mighty One's wisdom will blow into your heart like a warm and gentle breeze."

THE WISE:

A young man in the group called out, "Teacher, let us drink from your wisdom."

Others joined in saying, "Yes Teacher, give us your wisdom."

"What do you wish me to say to you?" said Elias.

The young man replied, "Tell us what wisdom is and how we can become wise."

The Teacher said, "I have no wisdom. God alone is wise. If you would drink of the Lord's Wisdom remember, true knowledge comes only from the Almighty. It is a gift given by the Lord and can be obtained from no other source. God gives Wisdom freely to the humble, but turns the prideful and self-righteous away empty-handed. When one's awe of God becomes greater than the fascination with Worldly things, this is the first step on the journey to Wisdom.

"The wise surround themselves with those who have a gentle and loving spirit, and they are numbered among them.

"Fools are ruled by their lower instincts. Chasing after worldly desires, their lives are driven into the ditch, leaving them stuck in the muck and mire of fleeting Worldly distractions.

"When searching for the Way that leads to the Eternal City, the wise rely upon God's Power to overcome their sins and cruelties. In their search for Wisdom, God reveals to them the Path that leads to the City of Peace, the New Jerusalem. The Lord shines His Light upon their path, leading them to Life Eternal.

"No matter how great the trials of life, in spite of the hardships that may lurk hidden and waiting to spring upon you, rejoice, for the Lord loves you. Trust in the Lord, for the Almighty holds the gift of never-ending life in His right hand. If you have faith in the Lord, the Mighty One will give you untold blessings and peace forevermore, replacing each tear with a smile, and every sorrow with joy.

"Do not blame Satan for your own sins and mistakes. The fallen human heart is errs, even without the Devil's temptations. Selfishness and cruelty come naturally to the Children of Eve and Adam. This is the curse carried by Adam's sons and daughters. Boldly confess your sins to the Blessed One, the Almighty, the Merciful. When you do, the Lord will save you from all evil and death.

"Satan and his demons are lost in their own darkness, never to be rescued, never to know God's mercy or joy. But our Merciful Father rescues His wayward human daughters and sons, placing their feet upon the Path that leads to the City of Peace.

"It is the Lord's will that you be saved from Satan's snares and traps. It is the Mighty One who will win your freedom from darkness and death. Trust in the Almighty and resist the Devil. Turn from darkness and walk into the Lord's marvelous Light."

THE BANQUET:

"God is like a king who invited all his subjects to a banquet. But only enemies, beggars, murderers and robbers accepted the invitation. Nonetheless, the king gave his finest wine and best food to those who came, waiting to eat until all his guests had ate and drank their fill. After everyone had feasted and drunk freely, the only food or drink remaining in the palace were dregs in the bottom of the wine jars. This is what the king feasted upon, happy that his guests were full and satisfied. The king's greatest desire was to benefit his people, even those who were unworthy and undeserving."

Elias taught until the sun hung low on the horizon. Most of those who had followed the Teacher out of the city returned to their homes for the night, but a few of us stayed and slept on the hillside next to him.

Rumors and tales about the Teacher multiplied with each passing day. Elias' fame made it difficult to appear in public without people flocking around him like a popular actor or poet. But the crowds were uncertain whether he was the star of a Euripidean tragedy or a comedy by Aristophanes. In spite of the multitudes of curiosity seekers, only a few honored Elias' teachings. Many critics and cynics jeered the Teacher and caused trouble wherever he went.

FOUR:
War and Violence

On a holiday honoring fallen warriors, we were walking with Elias in the agora. He was soon recognized and a crowd gathered. The growing parade of onlookers followed the Teacher until we came upon a civic ceremony honoring those who had fallen in battle. Elias stopped and listened to the ceremony. Soon the tag-along mob began to chant loudly, "Let the Teacher speak. Let the Teacher speak."

The orator could no longer be heard over the noise and commotion, interrupting the ceremony. Because they showed no sign of quieting, the speaker motioned for Elias to address the crowd, to silence them.

Climbing to the top of the platform the Teacher said, "My friends." The troublemakers began to quiet. Elias repeated again, "My friends." When the crowd became completely silent the Teacher said, "My dear friends, this gathering is not mine, nor is it yours. Why have you caused such a commotion? Let the memory of the dead be honored and the ceremony continue."

As the Teacher stepped away from the podium, the mob began to shout even more loudly than before, "Let the Teacher speak. Let the Teacher speak."

The official presiding over the ceremony said to Elias, "Please sir, say a few words to satisfy these troublemakers. Otherwise there will be a riot and the ceremony ruined."

Elias nodded. Taking the lectern once more he asked, "What would you have me say to you?"

On the platform sat a disabled warrior having several deep scars upon his face. The morning breeze pressed the garments against his legs showing them to be thin twigs, muscles shrunk, little more than skin and bone, the result of serious battle injuries. The disabled warrior spoke loudly and asked the Teacher, "We are engaged in a very costly and lengthy war. Is your god on our side, or does he favor our enemy?"

Elias said, "My dear, dear son, you ask the wrong question. The better question is: are we on the Lord's side?"

"Alright Teacher," said the former warrior. "Are we on your god's side? Is the Empire on your god's side in this war that now rages? Are we on the side of your god?"

The Teacher said, "Whenever peoples and nations march to war, they pray for their gods to accompany them into battle, to protect them and bring victory. Armies place religious symbols upon their shields, flags, standards, swords and uniforms – stars, crescent moons, and the graven images of gods and goddesses. Slogans are written upon military belts and embossed upon their helmets saying, 'May the gods be with us,' 'May Athena grant us victory,' or 'May Zeus deliver us.' These things are an abomination to the Almighty, the Creator, the One and Only. The Lord's favor and blessing do not rest upon those who use idols and magical talismans as protection, carrying graven images as good luck charms, superstitious emblems used to manipulate forces in the spiritual realm.

"The Lord's favor rests upon those who pursue justice, practice goodness, show mercy and offer forgiveness, even to their enemies. The Mighty One's favor is conferred upon those who possess gentle and loving hearts. The Lord's blessing is given to those who help and save the lost, aid widows and orphans, help strangers, give to the poor and comfort the sick. The Almighty's favor is upon those who busy themselves in giving hope to the hopeless, encouragement to the discouraged and aid to the oppressed, protecting those who cannot defend themselves. The Lord blesses those who minister peace in a World torn by strife, conflict, violence and suffering.

"War by definition injures and kills, multiplying injustice and tearing apart the social fabric of peace and love. God creates, but Satan destroys. War is the earthly embodiment of evil in this suffering World. The Lord's favor is not frequently or lightly granted to combatants engaged in violent acts against their brothers and sisters. War kills and destroys, but the Lord saves, gives life and builds up.

"The best that can be said about violent battle is this: In this present suffering and unjust World, there are times when war may appear the lesser of two evils. There are rare occasions when violence is a regrettable necessity, when going to battle for a just cause will produce less suffering, injustice and evil than allowing a demon-led army to inflict unrestricted abomination, injustice and cruelty upon the earth. But beware, for violence is not a favored or blessed endeavor of God. Going to war with just cause is a dangerous antidote to a fatal poison, a costly cure for a deadly disease. War is a harsh treatment that exacts a high price even in the best of circumstances. Going to war for a just cause is similar to amputating a gangrene-filled leg or arm. The surgeon rips, maims and disfigures, cutting off a needed appendage in the hope of stopping the disease to save the patient's life. But it is better never to have had gangrene at all, to walk upright in the light of the Lord's sun having both legs, hugging and embracing your brothers and sisters with two arms."

Many in the crowd became agitated as the Teacher spoke, incensed by his words. Some began to chant "Traitor," viewing Elias' words as disloyal to the Empire and to the warriors who sacrificed on the fields of battle.

Others in the crowd shouted their approval of Elias' words saying, "Blessed is he who comes in the name of the Lord. Blessed is the Teacher, a true prophet of God, peace be upon him."

The disabled veteran said, "Teacher, you have not answered my question. You have not told us whether this current war is just or unjust, good or evil, nor have you said whether your god is for us or against us in this conflict."

The Teacher looked down at the ground. Filled with sorrow he said, "The war that now rages in a far-away land seemingly has no end in sight. Thousands have died, including many of the Empire's soldiers. But most of the dead have been innocent men, women and children, citizens of the lands that our armies invaded. Untold treasure has been spent on arms and battle, money that could have fed the poor or been used to do great good. Because of this war, thousands of injured and suffering people in faraway lands utter the Emperor's name as a curse. What good has this war done? What benefit can be shown to justify the death and destruction? The Lord loves all people, even those living in faraway lands, not only Greeks, Judeans, Arameans, citizens of Antioch or the children of this Empire.

"The Lord sent Jonah to the blood-thirsty and pagan city of Nineveh. God had mercy even on that evil nation, when they repented of their sin with sackcloth and ashes. If the Almighty loved Nineveh, there is no doubt that God loves all cities and peoples.

"Let me ask you, my son, do you believe this war is something that a good, loving and compassionate God would bless and commend?"

Many in the crowd became enraged at these last words of the Teacher. Some walked away in disgust. Others yelled insults at Elias. One loud voice cried out, "A curse be upon the Teacher. False prophet! A curse be upon him and all his offspring for timeless ages. A blessing be upon anyone bold enough to shed his blood. May his blood be spilled upon the ground, where dogs will lap it and drink their fill.

Those upset by Elias's words began to scuffle with his supporters. We, his followers, climbed the platform and surrounded him, worried for his safety amid the conflict and unrest.

I said, "Teacher we should leave. It is not safe here."

He replied, "My friend, for those who speak the truth and serve the Lord, it is not safe anywhere upon the face of this imperfect World."

The disabled former warrior bitterly said to the Teacher, "Are you saying that my life has been wasted, that my sacrifice in battle was pointless, that I lost the use of my legs in pursuit of an unjust cause your god condemns? Is that what you are saying?"

The Teacher said, "My dear son, give ear to my words and listen carefully. You are a young man. Your life upon this earth has just begun. The Lord has not yet poured out His mercy upon you, but soon will, if you have faith in God's goodness."

The former warrior's expression changed from bitterness to one of deep sorrow. Tears began to well up within his eyes as he said, "Teacher, I would give anything to experience your god's mercy and to be used by the Lord, to do at least some good with my life."

The crowd was descending into chaos, taking on the look and appearance of a fight between rival gangs. The mob was no longer paying attention to the Teacher or to anyone on the platform, engulfed in conflict with one another.

Elias approached the young man and said to him quietly, "My son, at this very moment the Lord's mercy is available to you. The Almighty will do great things in your life, if you will simply have faith. Do you believe in God's mercy? Do you have faith that the Lord can heal you of the many hurts within your mind and soul?"

"Yes Teacher, I believe," said the former warrior.

FIVE:
Law and Peace

Elias said, "My son, I tell you to stand up and come with me from this place."

The clamor and unrest were so great, few noticed when the former warrior stood from his seat with his own spindly legs. Cautiously and haltingly, putting forward first his left leg, then the right, stooped and shaky he began to walk. With each step the former warrior became more upright, his path straightening and strengthening, his legs no longer mere sticks, but gaining bulk and strength with each step.

The Teacher said to the newly walking man, "Follow me, my son."

Descending down the back steps, the Teacher, his followers and the former warrior walked away from the unrest.

When the Imperial Guard arrived to restore order to the central agora, the mob was in full riot, looting the various stalls and shops.

A few days later, Elias was walking through the center of Antioch, near the palace. A wealthy, dignified and distinguished older man approached him saying, "Teacher, our Brotherhood works to restore holiness to our people. We uphold the Torah and call all God's Children to observe the forgotten and neglected traditions passed down to us by our forefathers. Will you join with us in calling the descendants of Israel back to holiness, so that God will make our nation great once more, restoring the glory of David's kingdom as in times of old?"

Elias did not immediately answer, but picked up an orange from a fruit-seller's cart. After examining the piece of fruit he replied, "My friend tell me, did you faithful obey the Torah and stringently honor the ancient traditions when you were a young man?"

He said, "Yes Teacher, I have always believed in the Torah and traditions handed down to us by our ancient fathers."

Elias said, "Dear friend, I did not ask if you believed in them. I asked if you practiced them when you were in your youth."

"I tried to Teacher," replied the man.

Elias asked, "Were you practicing the Torah when you got were drunk each day and despoiled a different maiden every night?"

The man's face turned red, like a pomegranate, as he tried to justify himself, "Even though I did not always do the right thing, I still knew right from wrong, which is more than today's immoral and degenerate younger generation can say."

Others belonging to the same religious party nodded their heads agreeing with the man saying, "Yes, we at least knew the difference between right and wrong."

"Friend, consider this orange," said the Teacher. "What do you think of its appearance?"

"It looks ripe and sweet," said the man.

Elias peeled the orange and handed him a slice saying, "Taste and see."

Biting into it the man's lips puckered. His face bent into a frown as he said, "Sour. This orange is exceedingly sour."

"It is the same with human beings," said the Teacher. "The outward appearance, the exterior facade, the actor's mask of morality and righteousness is of no importance, if the inside does not contain God's sweet goodness."

"Do you dare compare me and our party to this sour orange?" asked the man.

Elias said, "A person who knows what is right but chooses to do wrong, deserves no praise but only condemnation. Satan also knows the difference between right and wrong. Even though he knows the difference between good and evil, the Devil chooses to do what is wrong. Knowing the difference between good and evil, but choosing to do wrong, is the definition of sin.

"If a lawbreaker is ignorant of the law, how can she be severely punished for her ignorance? When there is no willful act of disobedience, the judgment must not be harsh.

"Those who know the Law, but willfully choose to disobey it, deserve a double portion of punishment. Those who know the Torah, but intentionally break having no regret for their transgressions, lawbreakers who deny their guilt, shall receive the harshest penalties of all. On the Last Day, when all are sentenced by the Almighty Judge, the prideful and unrepentant transgressors will be led away in chains to pay the full price of their crimes.

"My friend, when you were young, choosing to do wrong even though you knew what was right, in what way were you different from the Devil?

"Adam and Eve experienced nothing but blessings and goodness from the hand of the Lord, enjoying full fellowship and union with their Creator. In spite of knowing God's Goodness, they chose to believe the Serpent rather than their Father. My friend, it is not those who know God's Commands who stand approved. The justified are those who freely confess their transgressions, trusting in the Judge's mercy and love."

The man angrily turned and walked away saying to his party members, "This fellow is a false teacher, a wolf in sheep's skin, a deceiver. He is just another immoral revisionist, one more apostate who excuses idolaters, atheists, pagans, and Hellenists." The party members shook their heads in agreement and left.

Elias then said to those of us around him, "We must know the lessons of the past, and study the Lord's interaction with the Children of God recorded in Scripture. But do not have nostalgia for days gone by, as though answers to the World's problems can be found in the past. God shall reveal our salvation in the future. Redemption draws near. God's angels and the whole creation look longingly toward the day when all evil, sin and death are forever put away. The Lord's deliverance will one day be revealed. On that day all creatures will rejoice in God's mercy."

A young woman in the crowd said, "Teacher, what attitude should we have towards the Emperor? Should we revolt and establish godly rule?"

Looking intently into the woman's eyes Elias said, "My dear daughter, no matter what happens to this government or to the Emperor, nothing will bring back your brother from the grave, nor will revenge soothe the pain that now fills your heart."

Tears of anger appeared in the woman's eyes as she said, "But Teacher, it is an unholy and evil regime. The Emperor has killed thousands, not only my brother. Are we not justified to overthrow such evil and unjust leaders, so that good and godly government can be established?"

"My daughter, let me ask you a question," said Elias. "What price would you pay to prevent another young woman from losing her sibling, to save another sister from experiencing the pain that you have felt in losing your dear brother?"

"Teacher, I would give anything, sacrifice everything, even my own life, to prevent another woman from experiencing what I have gone through, and to prevent other parents from knowing the pain of losing their only son, as mine have."

"You are a good daughter and faithful sister," said Elias, touching the young woman's face with his finger, wiping a tear from her cheek the way a father would wipe tears from his beloved daughter's face. "Revolts and coups rarely produce the blessings hoped for at the beginning. Sowing the seeds of violent revolution too often produce an unexpected, unwelcome and unwanted crop of weeds. Countless wars and revolts have been started in the expectation of a quick and painless victory. Once the dogs of war are let loose, violence takes on a life of its own, visiting desolation upon all. Many revolts have been pursued in the name of justice and freedom. But untold terror, suffering, death and destruction are too often the result, as one tyrant is exchanged for another.

Revolutionary shouts of 'brotherhood, equality and freedom', are ruthlessly silenced by rebel leaders once they wield the executioner's sword. Cries of 'brotherhood, bread and freedom', are soon replaced by moans of mourning, violence begetting more violence, as death and destruction are let loose upon the land.

"Here is a hard saying for those who would receive it: The Almighty gives to each nation the leaders they deserve. If you desire just and merciful rulers, strive to be a just and merciful person. When a nation follows the Lord as their King, striving to live by God's Law of mercy and love, the Almighty confers upon that people increased freedom and justice. Remember, there is only one Leader worthy of our allegiance, the Lord. The Almighty is the only Ruler we must obey and worship."

A young man said, "But Teacher, you did not answer the woman's question. Should we revolt against the Emperor or not?"

Elias said, "All governments constructed by human hands are imperfect and filled with sin.

"Some governments are built upon the foundation of justice, mercy, good and right, but yet are deeply flawed and filled with wrongs. Perfect government does not exist in this fallen World. A nation's leaders are as sinful as the citizens they serve. To revolt against a government filled with manifold sins and errors, but founded upon righteous foundations will only bring catastrophe and sorrow. Governments founded upon solid foundations must be honored and preserved in spite of their many faults.

"Other governments are given to manifold errors, waste, folly, bribery and wrongs. To revolt against such a government may seem right, but beware. Revolution often gives birth to greater evil. In attempting to establish better rule, revolt may birth an evil regime, taking the nation from bad to worse.

"There is a third kind of government, evil by its very nature, having the Devil's disciple as its head. Filled with injustice and inhumanity, such a government is quick to shed innocent blood, enslave its people and practice every kind of depravity the human heart can invent.

It is the sacred duty for each Child of God to resist such evil leaders, to never help or aid the wrongs perpetrated by such an evil regime. All God's Children must resist and lay down their lives to stop such a demon led government."

The young man said, "Then Teacher, are you saying it is our holy obligation to rebel against the current evil and depraved Emperor?"

"My friend, the Lord's Children are never rebels," said Elias. "A person of faith strives to be kind, loving and just, even when all others are violent revolutionaries.

"Do not take up arms against your brothers and sisters. Murder cannot be overcome by more killing. Evil cannot be defeated by doing more evil. Violence is not stopped by shedding an enemy's blood upon the ground. Blood spilled upon the earth is not a pleasing sacrifice to God. The Lord hates bloodshed and murder. The Mighty One is the Father of all people. A loving father does not desire the death of a son or daughter, no matter how misguided or depraved they may have become. The Almighty despises violence, for hatred can only be overcome by love. Darkness is scattered by shining the Lord's Light upon it. Evil is defeated by goodness; and unforgiveness is conquered by God's Mercy.

"Evil can only endure for a short season, because it is empty and void, having no substance within itself. Hatred is the absence of love and darkness the lack of God's Light. When enveloped in blackness and stumbling in the night, darkness may seem all powerful, pervasive and foreboding. But when the night is pierced by a single sliver of light, darkness flees, because it has no substance within itself. Darkness cannot overcome the dimmest of lights. By its very nature the Lord's Light invades and overcomes the night. It can be no other way.

"To overcome an evil and dark ruler, God's Children shine forth God's Light, clearly showing the poverty and darkness of the evil regime for all to see, demonstrating that it is constructed of lies and delusions. When God's Children refuse to submit to the darkness, when they stand-up and oppose the Devil, even offering their bodies to be trampled, cut and beaten in the public square, when they show that their love for God and for others is so great that they willingly sacrifice their own bodies rather than submit to the darkness - this is when evil retreats to search for a more hospitable home.

"When the satanic rulers reveal their emptiness by killing God's Children, the light of truth starts to break forth and the winds of freedom begin to blow.

"Rebellion? Sheath your swords, my sons and daughters, or this present evil regime may be replaced by the hell of civil war, one evil despot replaced by another, the sling-shot exchanged for a dagger, the short-sword replaced by the arrow, catapults replacing spears, as death and darkness give birth to more darkness and death.

"Beware my children, for those who wield the sword and shed innocent blood shall be slaughtered with the same ruthless fury they let loose upon their brothers. Those who swing and slice with the knife, eagerly spilling the blood of others, shall themselves be cut and butchered. Those who throw the spear, gladly killing their brothers and sisters, shall be pierced and left to perish in the Desert of Sin, thirsty, lonely and alone."

"The time to resist this dark regime will come, but now is not the time nor is this the place."

Standing in the crowd were members of the Emperor's Secret Guard. When Elias first appeared in the Great Synagogue, the authorities watched him but were seemingly indifferent, viewing him as just another self-satisfied cleric spewing Jewish nonsense. As the Teacher's fame increased, dissention and unrest followed him wherever he went. Even though Elias preached against revolt and violence, he had no fear of the Emperor. This is intolerable to a tyrant, fear being a dictator's most important weapon, the one thing a despot cannot survive without.

Members of the Secret Guard now lurked in every crowd that gathered round the Teacher. They watched, listening carefully to his words, following him wherever he went, reporting whatever they saw and heard. In spite of their concerns about Elias, they still seemed unsure what to make of him or whether he posed a threat. But we never knew when the Teacher might be taken into custody, thrown into jail or worse.

SIX:
Breaking Bread

Gathered together to share the Sabbath meal Elias asked, "My friends, who do you believe me to be?"

Ishmael said, "Some say you are an angel of the Lord."

Eli said, "Others say you are a prophet sent by God."

Yousef said, "You are a wise philosopher."

Mariam said, "You are the most compassionate teacher the Lord has ever given to his people in Antioch."

I said, "Teacher, I cannot answer. Words fail me."

"Yutan, my friend, it is right to say nothing and to be silent about me. For I am only a servant," said Elias. "The Lord is everything, but I am nothing. The Almighty teaches, but I am only a sinful imperfect mouthpiece. You call me Teacher, but it is not I who teach. I have led you to the Eternal Spring. You drink deep from the Fountain where God's refreshing Waters flow. Your thirst is quenched by that which is not made by human hands or invented by an earthly mind. The words that fill your heart do not originate from the mouths of men or women."

One complained, "Teacher, why do you allow these women among us? Make them leave so we can concentrate upon your instruction and not be distracted by them."

Elias said, "Why do you speak ill of your sisters? All people are made in the Lord's image, women and men alike. The Almighty forms every baby in a woman's womb. The first loving heartbeat heard by each child is its mother's. Every man enters into the World by a woman, through water, blood, sweat and tears. A mother's breast feeds an infant its first taste of God's goodness. Children are taught to honor God while resting upon their mother's lap. No one is rejected by the Almighty, neither great nor small, man or woman, rich or poor, slave or free, Jew, Greek, Assyrian, Persian or Egyptian. Regardless of a person's station in life, all are equal in the Lord's eyes. Every man is our brother and each woman our sister, no matter the tribe or race. All are descendants of Eve and

Adam. Each old man is our father and every old woman our mother.

"God's Words are given to those who humbly receive them as hungry beggars accepting a loaf of bread. But the prideful and self-righteous reject the Almighty's Words. Beware, or you too may be numbered among the prideful and self-important fools who think themselves better than their sisters or brothers and too wise for the Lord's Wisdom."

THE STRIPES OF SUFFERING:

Elias took a loaf. Holding it high in his hands he said, "Do you see the dark brown stripes upon the bread, made by the oven's heat? Whenever you see these marks, may they remind you of the fires of testing and hard slavery God's Children endured in Egypt. Let these scars remind you of the persecutions suffered by the holy prophets, visited upon them by those who rejected God's Word. The prophets were beaten with whips and rods, leaving scars upon their backs. Whenever you see these stripes upon the bread, remember they are a sign given by the Almighty, a reminder that the Lord promises relief, rescue and reward to all God's Children held in bondage.

Remember the words of the prophet, 'by His stripes we are healed.'

"The Mighty One promises a crown of glory and a place of honor to all who suffer for the cause of mercy and love. The Children of Light are often rejected. But the Lord's deliverance is always near and close at hand.

"My friends, look again at this bread. Made of grain from a thousand different stocks, it is united together into a single loaf. You too were gathered from many different families and tribes, but are now joined together into one fellowship. You are the Lord's dear sons and daughters.

"My brothers and sisters, do you see this loaf? It is one and united." Then he broke it into small parts, handing a piece to each person present. "The loaf was united as one, but now is torn apart. Tonight we are joined as one, but soon we will be scattered to the four corners of the earth. This is done that the seeds of God's Word may be spread and planted both near and far. When the day of scattering comes, do not mourn. Do not weep when I am separated from you. Do not be sad when you are torn away from your brothers and sisters. This must happen to fulfill God's plan. Like seeds we must all be scattered and planted into the earth, so that a heavenly harvest may be gathered from many fields, both near and far, in Rome, Corinth, Thessalonica, Alexandria,

Damascus, Galatia, Ephesus and beyond, to far away fields where Godly synagogues will be established to teach the Word of the Lord.

One day the Anointed One will come. He will distribute not only bread, but also his flesh. On that day the blood of the Passover Lamb will be poured upon the Children of God, washing away your sin and marking you for salvation, just as Hebrew homes were marked by the lamb's blood in Egypt saving them from the Angel of Death.

"Let us thank God for this meal the Lord has provided. 'When I behold the Heavens and the work of Your hands, the moon and the stars that You set in place, what are mere humans that You are mindful of them, mortals that You take note of them?'

"'Blessed are You Lord our God, Ruler of the Cosmos, who brings forth bread from the earth.'

"Mighty One, use all who are seated here to distribute Your Spiritual Bread to the starving masses. Like seeds planted in the earth, we too have sprouted and sprung forth from the ground. Almighty Lord, may we be fruitful and multiply, freely providing Your Spiritual Food to all who hunger, just as You have fed and nourished us. Amen." We then shared the meal.

THE WAY TO LIGHT AND THE DARK ROAD:

After dinner Elias reclined and began to teach. "Be diligent," he said. "Persevere and let no one lead you astray from the Way of Light. Difficult and rocky is the path that leads to Light and Life.

"The Way of Light is difficult because it is the path of humility and sacrifice. But the road of darkness and death is easy, for it is the path of pride, selfishness and self-indulgence.

"Those traveling upon the road to darkness and death serve only themselves, caring little for the Almighty or for others. They are strangers to love, compassion and mercy. Refusing to confess their sins and misdeeds, they conceal and excuse their many wrongs.

"Those walking in the Way of Light and Life are filled with love for God and for others. Willingly they sacrifice, giving even their own lives for their brothers and sisters. Aware that they are sinners and lost apart from the Almighty, knowing their unworthiness, they eagerly confess their evil deeds, relying upon the Lord's mercy and forgiveness.

"If you are able, carry the entire burden of the Lord's Commands. It is a lighter load than the World's burden of darkness and death. But if you are unable to bear the full weight, carry what you are able, trusting in the Lord's love and mercy to save you from sin and death.

"There are two paths: the Way to Light and Life, and the road to darkness and death.

"The Way of Light is this: Hear O Children of Israel, the Lord is God and there is no other. Serve only God and worship no other. Love the Lord, your Creator, and love your brothers and sisters. Love even those who do you harm, for they too were created by the Almighty. They too are the Lord's Children, even though they have gone astray and rebelled against God.

"Freely give to those in need. The Mighty One gives generous gifts to the Children of Light that they may generously share their riches with others. Blessed are those who freely and generously give good gifts to their sisters and brothers.

DARKNESS OF THE DEEP:

"The World is a raging river. When the current sweeps you away from shore, dragging you under the surface enveloping you in the darkness of the deep, do not struggle against the evil flow or you will surely drown.

Have faith, pray to the Lord, hold your breath and save your strength. The deadly current cannot maintain its grasp upon the Children of Light. God will make it spit you safely onto solid ground, just as Jonah was delivered from the sea by a great fish that dropped him upon the sandy shore.

"If you have faith, you too will be saved from the darkness of the deep and safely deposited upon a sandy beach. Afterwards you will praise God for His deliverance from the watery pit. You will walk upon the shore, not only saved but also bathed, the Old Adam and Eve drowned in the cleansing waters, but the New Man and Woman raised and reborn to never-ending Life."

IMPORTANT THINGS:

A young woman said, "Teacher, please do not stop. We want to hear more."

Many of us agreed saying, "Yes Teacher, tell us more."

"Very well," said Elias. "The days of a person's life are few, soon gone, never to return again. Do not waste precious moments pursuing things that have little importance. If an endeavor has no eternal significance, it is also unimportant today. Only two things have never-ending value, the Lord, and your brothers and sisters. All else will pass away in the blink of an eye and soon be forgotten."

CHILDREN OF GOD:

Miriam said, "But Teacher, who are our brothers and sisters? Is it only our families and those who belong to the Tribes of Israel?"

Elias asked, "Who were the first man and woman?"

"Adam and Eve, peace be upon them," said Miriam.

"Are all human beings descended through them?"

"Yes Teacher."

"Where did Adam and Eve come from?"

"They were created by the Lord."

"What did the Mighty One call them?"

"His children," said Miriam.

"In whose image were Adam and Eve made?" asked the Teacher.

"God's."

Elias said, "If Adam and Eve were made by the Lord and formed in the Image of the Almighty, if all people are descendants of Eve and Adam, and if every person is a Child of God, then who is our sister or brother?"

"Every man and woman," said Mariam

"Well said my daughter. You are right. All people are our sisters and brothers. The right way to treat our siblings is with never ending love and forgiveness."

PARADISE:

"My friends, you are God's Children and should have no fear of death. The end of life in this World is a terror only to those who have no faith in the Lord. When a Child of God dies, Paradise is theirs. The Almighty's angels swiftly carry them to their heavenly home, where they are surrounded by God's Presence, enveloped in the Almighty's Mercy and given rest in the Bosom of Abraham, peace be upon him.

"Only Children of Esau should fear death's arrival. Esau sold his birthright for a bowl of stew, obeying his belly rather than the Lord. Many in this World are like their father Esau, trading their inheritance as God's Children for things that momentarily fill the stomach but starve the soul.

"Those who have faith in God have overcome the World. They obey the Lord rather than their belly, fearing neither death nor any terror belonging to this dark age."

CHILDREN OF LIGHT AND DARK RULERS

"In this present age of darkness God's Children are subjected to many afflictions and tests. The dark rulers of this fallen World hate God's offspring. But for the Lord's Children the troubles of this World are brief and temporary trials. The Children of Light are strangers to this current kingdom, aliens who long to return to their native land, the Kingdom of Light. There all God's Children will dwell with the Almighty for timeless ages."

THAT WHICH IS RIGHT:

Elias said, "Do that which is right and flee from all forms of evil:
"Love and worship the Lord without ceasing.
Utter no curses, speak only blessings, tell no gossip.
Do good to your father, mother, brothers and sisters.
Do not kill or raise an arm in anger against another.

Forgive all people and do not seek revenge.

Be faithful, merciful and loving to your spouse.

Do not steal, cheat or do any form of injustice.

Let no lie or deceit pass your lips.

Do not desire another's possessions or be greedy.

Be humble, resisting all forms of arrogance and pride.

Be compassionate, giving generous alms to the needy.

CONCLUSION:

"The road to darkness and death is littered with all manner of greed, pride, injustice, violence, selfishness, murder, hatred, theft, falsehood, slander, deceit and lust.

"The Way of Light and Life is paved with love for the Lord and for all people, doing that which is good, right, compassionate and merciful."

Late in the evening, Elias had finished teaching when a loud knock was heard.

Opening the door a young man asked me, "Is the Teacher inside? I must speak with him." It was a soldier dressed in full armor.

SEVEN:
Midnight Warning

The young man's uniform was that of the Imperial Guard, those specially selected by the Emperor to watch and protect his person, palace and the Imperial Family. Tongue-tied I stood motionless, not wanting to utter a lie, but fearful to admit that Elias was seated inside. Whatever the reason for his visit, I assumed it must be to work some sort of mischief. What good has the Imperial Guard ever done? More than mere bodyguards, the Emperor wielded them as his bloody iron fist, using them to carry out his most violent atrocities.

Elias said, "Yutan, let the young man enter. Have him come and rest his feet for a while."

Hearing the Teacher's words, I began to see the guard through new eyes, looking beyond the uniform, no longer seeing a fierce and ruthless assassin. Not far beyond his youth, the man's boyish face was in stark contrast to the fierce armor, weapons and insignia that he wore. Perhaps his heart and soul were not as evil as his outward uniform suggested. I swung open the door and motioned for him to enter.

Elias said, "Come in my son. Welcome. Here, sit down beside me. Would you like something to eat or perhaps a drink?"

Taking a seat on a stool next to the Teacher, the Guard sat erect, stiff, formal and wooden. Having a stony expression upon his face that betrayed no emotion he said, "No thank-you sir."

I had never been this close to a member of the Imperial Guard before, having only seen them from a distance. Stories and rumors about their violent deeds were a constant subject of discussion throughout the Capital.

"What can I do for you, my son?" Elias asked the young man. "You asked for me."

"Teacher, I have come to you at great risk to my own safety," said the Guard.

I thought, "You are not the only one who feels at risk."

He continued, "I had to come to you, Teacher, to warn you."

"Warn me of what son?" said Elias.

"I am one of the Emperor's personal guardians, one of those responsible for his safety. I stand watch inside his quarters as one of the Imperial Highness' bodyguards. Often I overhear his conversations with high officials."

These words only increased my fear. I wondered, "Why would one of the Emperor's personal bodyguards come here to speak with Elias? What kind of trick is this?"

"Today while standing at my post," said the soldier, "Archon Menelaus came to speak with the Emperor, together with several members of his Council of Elders. They came to discuss you, Teacher, and were very upset.

"Archon Menelaus said to the Emperor, 'Your Highness, the situation in the city cannot continue. This man whom the ignorant and uneducated crowds call the Teacher, is causing great unrest in the synagogues and throughout the city, even causing disruptions in the agora. You must take action Majesty.

"'Must,' asked the Emperor challenging the Archon's demand.

"'Yes must, your Highness, to avoid rebellion and to maintain order in the city. This Teacher is a threat,' said Menelaus.

"'A threat to you perhaps, but I see little cause for alarm,' said the Emperor.

"The Archon replied, 'Your Highness, the people have begun to discuss insurrection with this Teacher.'

"The Emperor's expression and demeanor changed when he heard this. Before, he seemed bored and annoyed by the Archon and Elders, indifferent to their words, appearing to pay only partial attention. But now the Emperor turned and looked at the Archon with a hint of anger in his eyes saying, 'Rebellion... is that true? Menelaus, did you hear this with your own ears, or is this another of your pathetic attempts to manipulate me into doing your own bidding?'

"'Your Highness,' said the Archon, 'the people have spoken to the Teacher about rebellion on numerous occasions.' Waving his hand towards the Elders he said, 'We have all heard these conversations with our own ears.' The Elders shook their heads in agreement.

"The Emperor paused as he looked intently into the eyes of the Archon, as though sizing him up and considering his words. Then he broke into a smile and said, 'Oh, you are far too dower and serious, Menelaus.

You really must get out of the House of Prayer more often and enjoy yourself a little. Go to the gymnasium or the theatre. Have a little fun. There is no need to be concerned about a little trifle like this Teacher, no reason at all. Do not worry, my dear pious friend. I will address this small problem, no need to concern yourself with this matter any longer, no need at all.'

"'Then you will deal with the Teacher?' asked the Archon.

"'Do not worry, my friend,' said the Emperor. 'It is a small matter, very small indeed.'

"Satisfied, the Archon and Elders left. Then the Emperor called for the Commander of the Imperial Guard and said, 'The next time this Teacher appears outside the House of Prayer, arrest him.'

"'Yes sir,' said the Commander.

"'On the steps outside the House of Prayer, mind you, not inside. Place your best men in the side streets near the House of Prayer. I will have members of the Secret Guard hidden among the crowds as well. When this Teacher is spotted, take hold of him. Do not let him enter the House of Prayer. Mind you, he must not slip through your hands or it will not go well for you. Do you follow?'

"The Commander saluted and said, 'I live to serve the Empire and your Imperial Highness.'"

Elias betrayed no emotion, appearing unmoved by the soldier's words.

I asked the Guard, "And why is it you have graced us with such important information? Why would a member of the Imperial Guard care what happens to the Teacher, or to any of us?"

The young man's expression changed, looking like a shamed boy caught stealing cakes from a windowsill where they were placed to cool. Looking down at the floor he said to Elias with guilt in his voice, "Yes, we who are members of the Imperial Guard are feared, and for good reason. We have done much violence and evil." Then looking up into Elias's eyes he said, "But Teacher, I too am a Jew, belonging to the Tribe of Judah, and have heard you teach. I believe your words. Believe mine now. If you are arrested, there is nothing I or anyone else can do to help you. Please do not go near the Great House of Prayer." Then the Guard stood up from the seat, placed his helmet upon his head, saluted Elias and left.

Many of us had a fitful rest that night, but Elias appeared to sleep soundly. The next morning we arose, washed our faces, hands and feet, and ate the morning meal. Then Elias said, "Come, we must go to Great House of Prayer."

EIGHT:
The Emperor

Surprised I said, "Teacher, do you not remember the young man's warning. It is not safe. Besides, it is not even the Sabbath. Why must we go today?"

"Those who serve God experience times of danger, and travel through many hazardous places, but the Lord's work goes on without fear," said Elias.

The Teacher had made up his mind and would not be deterred. But fear and dread enveloped me. I was tempted to let him go to the Great House alone, afraid for my own safety. Then the image came into my mind's eye of Elias being seized by the Emperor's men, just another person added to the countless "disappeared ones", those seized by the authorities but never heard from again. To never see Elias again nor to hear his voice, to never give him a respectful burial, or even to know where his body had been thrown - the thought of these things seemed unbearable to me. So, without further protest, I readied myself to accompany the Teacher to the Great House. The others also put on their cloaks and sandals, resigned to whatever dangers the day might bring.

Nearing the Great Synagogue, Elias's followers tightly surrounded him in a protective circle. When we entered the square in front of the Great House, members of the Secret Guard descended upon us from all sides and members of the Imperial Guard also approached, quickly surrounding us.

Ishmael, the others and I, stood between Elias and those who drew near. We intended to hinder and delay them long enough for the Teacher to make an escape. But when the Imperial Guard came close Elias said, "My brothers and sisters, do not prevent these men from carrying out their orders. My friends, do not seek to overcome evil by wielding the same tools of violence that the Enemy uses. If you do, Satan will master and defeat you."

"But Teacher," I protested, "they intend to harm you."

Elias said, "The intentions of evil men and women are of little consequence to the Almighty, or to the Children of Light. The Children of Darkness are like tumbleweeds carried about by every wisp of the wind, blown to and fro by the morning breeze, dead, rootless and having no good purpose. Do not fear them, for even the winds of strife are subject to the Lord's command. My friends, let these men do their duty." Reluctantly we let the Guard approach Elias.

The Commander said, "Teacher, we must escort you, and your companion Yutan, to the Imperial Palace."

"Very well my son," said Elias, "carry out your orders."

To hear that the authorities knew my name and that I was to be arrested with the Teacher, sent a shiver of fright down my spine. Horrors flashed through my mind, thoughts of torture, pain and death, as I prayed for just one more opportunity to tell my family that I loved them. Regret filled my heart for not expressing my affection more often. But the thing I feared most was disappointing Elias or betraying him because of my weakness.

The Imperial Guard took us into custody. They marched us through the streets of Antioch until we came to the main gate of the Imperial Palace.

After waiting for many hours, the guards then escorted us into a large room that was filled with enticing and delectable aromas. In the center was a huge banqueting table. Occupying every available space were delicacies from all over the Empire - roast pork, steamed crab, fried crocodile, various sea creatures, pomegranates, dates, figs, nuts, oranges, grapes and large pitchers of unmixed wine.

The Emperor was reclining beside the table, eating and drinking. In private the people called Antiochus IV many derisive names. Some referred to him as Belial, the Son of Iblis or the Beast. Instead of his chosen title "Epiphanes" (meaning God-manifest), many called him "Epimanes" (meaning the mad).

The Emperor motioned to us and said, "Please my honored guests, be seated."

Two servants directed us to recline upon couches across the table from Antiochus.

"Friends, please eat," said the Emperor. "Feast upon anything you want. Have as much as your heart desires, until your stomachs are full."

I very much wanted a few grapes to munch upon, but felt guilty to accept anything if the Teacher was not eating or drinking. After all, we were in an unholy house, a pagan palace, and these foods were unclean.

The Emperor said, "Teacher, I have heard so much about you and greatly desire to share in your knowledge. Please speak and let me drink from your well of wisdom, just as others have. With the aid of your wise words I could do many good and wonderful things for the Empire and for your people. I greatly covet your help in ruling my kingdom."

Elias sat directly across from the Emperor, silent and emotionless, showing no reaction to his words.

Antiochus continued, "Do you not wish to share your knowledge with me? No? Well, I can see your point. After all, I am a terrible sinner and am unworthy of your gods' wisdom. This I freely admit. It is true that I am ruthless with my enemies. But it must also be noted that I am extremely generous and lenient with my friends."

Elias still betrayed no emotion, not uttering a single syllable, sitting silently while staring intently at the Emperor.

"Well then Teacher," said Antiochus, "since you are hesitant to speak, let me tell you a story of my own.

THE WISE FOX

"There once was a very wise fox who visited the farmer's property every day. This fox would go to the farmer's chicken pen and speak to the hens. The chickens, being pea-brained, would become stirred into a frenzy by the fox's words. The hens would leave their eggs unattended and begin to flap their wings. Some tried to escape from the pen because of the unrest caused by the fox. The roosters would get into conflict, ripping and tearing each other, disagreeing whether the fox was good or evil. This went on for some time. Every day the wise fox would come to speak to the chickens. Each day the chickens and roosters would fly into a frenzy and become distressed.

"The farmer said to himself, 'This cannot continue. It must be stopped. Even though the pen is strong and the chickens can never escape, this fox is disrupting egg production and is making the hens lose weight. The chickens will not be ready for slaughter at the appointed time, and the roosters are injuring one another.'

"The next day the farmer went to the chicken pen and waited for the fox's arrival. When he came the farmer said, 'Oh fox, you are exceedingly wise and I greatly respect all your knowledge. But I cannot allow you to distress my chickens any longer. If I find you disturbing my chickens ever again, I shall take my bow and pierce your heart with an arrow. But wise fox, I also have some very good news. You are welcome to come live in my farmhouse, feast at my table and enjoy all the delectable delicacies my farm produces. Not only that, but I will give you many other favors as well. Indeed wise fox, I will give you everything your heart desires. All you must do to receive these many blessings from my hand is to stop distressing the chickens and come dwell inside my beautiful home.'

THE ULTIMATUM

"Teacher," said the Emperor, "that is the end of my story. Admittedly it is very poor and unwise in comparison to your wisdom. But please honor me with your opinion. What do you think? If you were the wise fox, how would you answer the farmer?"

Elias still sat motionless, not uttering a word, staring at the Emperor betraying no emotion.
"Well there is no need to give me your answer today," said Antiochus. "Go your way. Think well upon it and come back tomorrow to give me your opinion."

THE TEACHER'S RESPONSE

Elias then rose from his seat. I was surprised when he finally spoke. Looking directly at the Emperor the Teacher said, "The abomination of desolation predicted by the Prophet will soon take place just as foretold. But woe to the man who does this evil deed. The mark of destruction will rest upon him and his throne; and he will pay the full price for his sins.

"In spite of careful preparations and ruthless savagery, his wicked plans will come to nothing. The abomination shall soon be removed and the holiness of Zion be restored.

"In thirty-five-times-seven a second abomination shall be visited upon the Holy Temple, when not a single stone shall remain upon another. This will take place after the Anointed One has come and completed his purpose. The second abomination will remain and last until the End of Days."

For a brief moment the Emperor seemed disoriented, having a look of worry upon his face. Quickly regaining his composure Antiochus tersely said to his servants, "Show the Teacher out."

As we left the Imperial Palace, Elias did not utter another word. We walked silently through the streets of Antioch soon arriving at my house where Elias's followers had returned.

Entering through the door Elias said, "Come my friends, let us spend the night outside the city, under the stars. There we can rest in peace"

NINE:
Night Descends

Once outside the city walls we made our beds under a tree. After sharing a dinner of bread and dried fish we reclined together around the fire.

Elias recited,
"By the rivers of Babylon we sat,
sat and wept,
remembering Zion.
There on the willows
we hung our harps.
Our captors required of us songs.

Our oppressors asked for songs of joy saying,
'Sing us one of the Songs of Zion.'
But how can we sing songs of God in a foreign land?"

The Teacher said, "My dear friends, I am weary and worn out, fatigued to the sinews and marrow, to the very depth of my soul. It is a dark night and the moon has hidden itself from view. I am weary of the wrongs that evil men do in nighttime shadows. Soon those who love the dark, those who oppress the Lord's people and who steal bread from the mouths of the poor, will seek to extinguish the small portion of God's Light that has been given to me. But I have faithfully shown forth the Lord's Light and it shall continue to shine in the night. God has used me to illumine the deeds of darkness, and they can no longer remain hidden from view. It is for this reason that those who love the dark now desire to put out the Light.

THE PROMISED LAND

"Like the Prophet Moses, peace be upon him, I have climbed to the mountaintop and have seen the Glory of the Lord. Everything the Mighty One has whispered into my ear I have faithfully spoken to you, my dear friends. The spark of God's Spirit has come upon you, like a raging fire, the Spirit of the Prophets. The Light of the Prophets has illumined your hearts casting out the darkness, placing upon you a flame that no evil rain can dampen or extinguish. Though a black night descend, desiring to douse the Fire, as the Light advances the darkness must recede and retreat, for the night is unable to resist or defeat the Almighty's power. Even though a demon wind blow and bluster, seeking to snuff out my earthly breath, the Lord's Lamp has become a bright blaze lighting your way in the darkness.

"God's Truth has been given to you. You are a people of the Light. The Lord's Torch shines forth, leading you to the Anointed One, the Completion, the Omega, the Crown of the Prophets. Watch and wait patiently for his coming. After him, there will be no need for further illumination. He shall shine forth the Great Light, dispelling and defeating all darkness and death. In him all will find the Light and Life of the Almighty.

"Just as Moses climbed Mount Nebo and viewed the Promised Land, I too have seen the other side, a land flowing with milk and honey, the place of the Lord's Promise, a land where all God's Children will be bathed in Light and dwell with the Almighty for timeless ages.

But like Moses, I will not be there when our nation steps out of darkness and into the Lord's Marvelous Light."

Hearing this, voices of confusion arose as one said to another, "What does the Teacher mean? Is he going to travel abroad to another land? Is he going to Egypt or to the Holy Temple in Jerusalem? Why does the Teacher say he will not be with us when the Light of God's Truth shines upon our nation? What does he mean by this?"

Elias raised his arms to quiet the murmuring, "My dear brothers and sisters, do not let your hearts be troubled, neither let them be afraid. It is a dark and moonless night; and it will grow darker before the break of Dawn. But the night is long spent and the Sunrise shall soon come."

Miriam said, "Please Teacher, tell us plainly. We do not understand what you are saying."

"My dear friends, soon I will no longer with you, but you must remain courageous and strong. I am happy tonight, oh so happy. Even though my body is weary and fatigued to the bone, the Mighty One has given me sufficient peace to face tomorrow's evil. I have seen the Promised Land and have beheld the Glory of the Lord. One day we shall all be united in the Bosom of Abraham. In Elysian Fields we will walk arm-in-arm as sisters and brothers, walking together in the Shining Light of the Lord's Presence, having no darkness or shadow within or without.

"Tomorrow you will be tested, but you must stand firm. No mere man can kill the Almighty or extinguish the Lord's Light. Be of good cheer and be bold. Wrong cannot overcome Right. The sound of war and violence cannot drown out the Lord's Peaceful Voice. No weapon fashioned against us in Heaven above or in Hades below can defeat the Power of God's Word.

"My friends, freedom will reign - if not today, then tomorrow it shall. If the Lord's freedom does not envelop the World now, it will reign within your hearts waiting for the day that Eternal Truth stands victorious. Until that day, may the Lord's Will be done, regardless the hardship and no matter the cost. Amen."

Worried by Elias's words, none of us dared ask the Teacher another question. Exhausted, we laid our bodies upon makeshift beds, resting under the drooping branches of a weeping willow. But the sweet release of sleep evaded us, for we feared the coming of the dawn.

Arising the next morning Elias said, "Come my friends, it is time for Sabbath prayers. We must worship at the Great House of Prayer."

TEN:
The Great House of Prayer

I wanted to say, "Teacher, could we not miss prayer just this one Sabbath?" But the words would not form in my mouth. No one uttered a sound of protest. We simply followed Elias in silence.

As we walked to the Great House, I gazed intently at the Teacher's face. It had the look of sorrow upon it. Perhaps Elias was afraid too. But if he was, determination seemed his overriding emotion, as though he had a task to do and nothing was going deter him from completing it, his chin set forward and jaw clenched tightly against whatever the day might bring.

Following the Teacher, we neared the Great House of Prayer, arriving after worship had already begun. Elias climbed the stone steps leading to the main entrance, the rest of us surrounding him closely. A man approached the Teacher and bowed, wanting to stop and speak with him.

Mariam stepped in front of the young man saying, "I am sorry, the Teacher is already late…" trying to prevent him from delaying Elias.

The young man pushed Mariam aside and drew near to the Teacher. Raising his arm, the man forcefully drove it down upon him. As he did a piece of metal glistened in the morning sunlight. The dagger reached its target, driving deep into Elias's chest, his tunic quickly turning from bright white to rose red.

Before any of us could react, the young man drove another swift and hard thrust into Elias's breast. "Clang, clang, clang," the bronze dagger dropped. Falling down the stone steps, the blade making another "clang" with each step it struck. The attacker turned and fled, soon disappearing into the crowd.

I tried to catch Elias as he crumpled, but merely succeeded in slowing his fall, easing his impact upon the stone, blood now running down the steps, following the same path the dagger had trod moments before.

Elias cried out, "The House of Prayer. Take me into the House of God. I must offer my worship there."

Several of us carried him up the remaining steps and through the tall doors into the Holy House. As always, it was filled with the scent of incense, carrying the prayers of the faithful to God. Rays of sunlight shown upon the smoke as the assembly sang psalms of praise, giving the House of Prayer the otherworldly look and sound of Heaven itself.

We intended to lay Elias down in the back of the Great House and call for a physician's help, but the Teacher said, "No, take me to the front."

Pushing our way down the aisle, at first few worshippers paid attention to us, not knowing about the attack on the synagogue's steps. Many turned and looked as we carried the Teacher to the front.

We were going to lay Elias down just outside the Holy Place, but the Teacher said, "No, place me upon the Altar of Incense."

Several clerics tried to stop us from approaching the Holy Place, but we would not be deterred. It was our Teacher's request. We were not going to refuse him anything, not now. Pushing through the throng of clerics and Levites, we drew near to the ark that held the Holy Scriptures, the altar of incense laying just below it. Gently placing Elias upon the altar, his blood flowed down upon the white stone, staining it. The red liquid fell in huge drops from the alabaster altar onto the marble floor, each drip making a sound as it splashed.

I tightly grasped Elias's right hand, looking deeply into his eyes.

He said to me, "Thank-you, my dear friend." Seeing the tears running down my face he said, "Do not mourn for me, my brother. This is what must be. This is how evil will be overcome by Good. Evil kills and Good dies, sacrificed upon the altar to pay the price for sin. This is how the Anointed One will deliver God's Children from death to Life. In the fullness of time, the sacrificial Lamb of God will be offered up.

"We all must be willing to suffer, willing to die for the right and for the Good, for the sake of God's Truth and for our brothers and sisters.

"Do not hate the one who has done this act of violence against me. He has only killed himself, not me. He is to be pitied, not despised. I forgive him and those who sent him. You also must forgive, my dearest friend, and harbor no hint of bitterness within your soul."

The altar was now surrounded, not only by Elias's followers, but by Levites and the various worshippers attending the Great House that day. Prayer had stopped and the entire assembly was standing round the Altar.

Elias let go of my hand and stretched his arm skyward, his palm covered in red, smeared with his own blood.

Looking straight up, it was as though he were seeing beyond the decorated dome, past the blue tiles and mosaics, through the roof, beyond the clouds and into Heaven itself. Then he cried out, the words echoing round the walls, "Oh God... Take my hand, precious Lord."

The breath of life then left Elias' lungs. His arm fell and his body went limp.

A man standing nearby witnessing these events asked, "Who was this man?"

I replied, "The Teacher said he was nothing, but to me was everything. He was a humble servant who pointed the way to God."

38924387R00068

Made in the USA
Charleston, SC
19 February 2015